Collins

EARTHQUAKES
AND VOLCANOES

FASCINATING FACTS

D1147854

Published by Collins
An imprint of HarperCollins Publishers
Westerhill Road
Bishopbriggs
Glasgow G64 2QT
www.harpercollins.co.uk

First published 2013
Second edition 2016

© HarperCollins Publishers 2013
Maps © Collins Bartholomew Ltd 2013

Collins® is a registered trademark of HarperCollins Publishers Ltd

All rights reserved. No part of this publication may be reproduced, stored in a retrieval system, or transmitted, in any form or by any means, electronic, mechanical, photocopying, recording or otherwise without the prior permission in writing of the publisher and copyright owners.

The contents of this publication are believed correct at the time of printing. Nevertheless the publisher can accept no responsibility for errors or omissions, changes in the detail given or for any expense or loss thereby caused.

HarperCollins does not warrant that any website mentioned in this title will be provided uninterrupted, that any website will be error free, that defects will be corrected, or that the website or the server that makes it available are free of viruses or bugs. For full terms and conditions please refer to the site terms provided on the website.

A catalogue record for this book is available from the British Library

ISBN 978-0-00-816927-5

10 9 8 7 6 5 4 3 2

Printed in China by R R Donnelley APS Co Ltd.

All mapping in this book is generated from Collins Bartholomew digital databases.
Collins Bartholomew, the UK's leading independent geographical information supplier, can provide a digital, custom, and premium mapping service to a variety of markets.
For further information:
Tel: +44 (0)208 307 4515
e-mail: collinsbartholomew@harpercollins.co.uk
Visit our website at: www.collins.co.uk   www.collinsbartholomew.com

If you would like to comment on any aspect of this book, please contact us at the above address or online.
e-mail: collinsmaps@harpercollins.co.uk

MIX
Paper from
responsible sources

FSC
www.fsc.org   FSC C007454

FSC™ is a non-profit international organisation established to promote the responsible management of the world's forests. Products carrying the FSC label are independently certified to assure consumers that they come from forests that are managed to meet the social, economic and ecological needs of present and future generations, and other controlled sources.

Find out more about HarperCollins and the environment at
www.harpercollins.co.uk/green

Contents

Dates in this publication are based on the Christian Era and the designations BC and AD are used throughout. These designations are directly interchangeable with those referring to the Common Era, BCE and CE respectively.

Introduction

Earthquakes and volcanoes are some of the most exciting and most dangerous natural features on our planet. The Earth can seem solid and unchanging to us but this book reveals how the huge rocky plates that make up the Earth's crust are constantly reshaping the surface of our world. Small movements of the Earth's plates cannot be felt but despite this they still make massive changes to the surface of the Earth over a long time. The movements cause earthquakes and feed volcanic eruptions, reminding us that we live on the very thin surface of a planet with red-hot, molten rock inside. Earthquakes and volcanoes are all part of the natural change of our planet, but to those who live in risk zones these events happen suddenly, creating a devastating amount of destruction to people and landscapes.

Inside Earth

Our planet, Earth, is made up of three main layers called the crust, mantle, and core. The crust, the outermost layer, is rigid and very thin compared with the other two. Beneath the oceans, the crust varies little in thickness, generally extending only to about 5 km. The thickness of the crust beneath the continents is much more variable but averages at about 30 km, and under large mountain ranges, such as the Alps or the Sierra Nevada, the base of the crust can be as deep as 100 km. The Earth's crust is brittle and can break. It is made up of separate pieces called plates. These are always moving and earthquakes and volcanoes often occur at the points where they meet. Below the crust, the mantle is a dense, hot layer of semi-solid rock approximately 2,900 km thick. At the centre of the Earth lies the core, the inner part of which is solid.

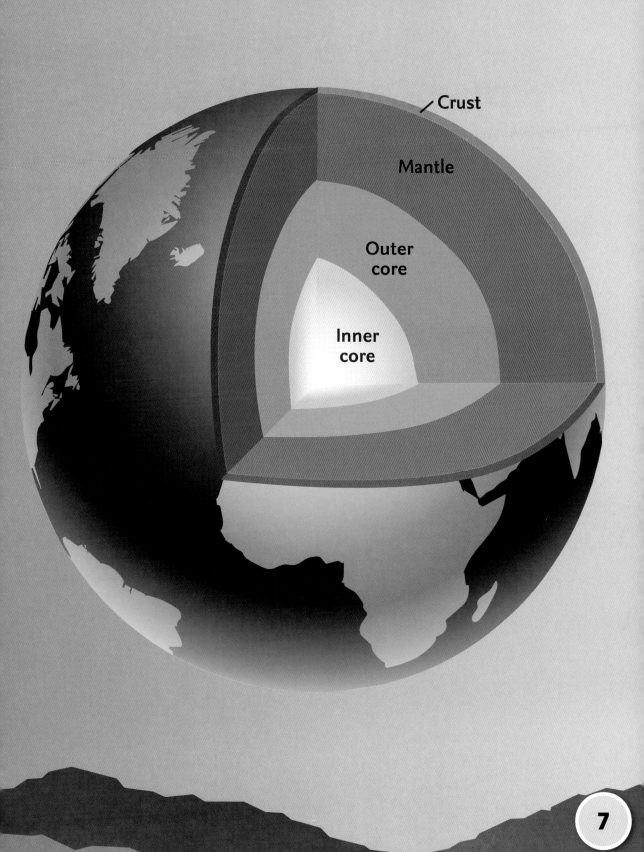

Crust

Mantle

Outer
core

Inner
core

Plate tectonics

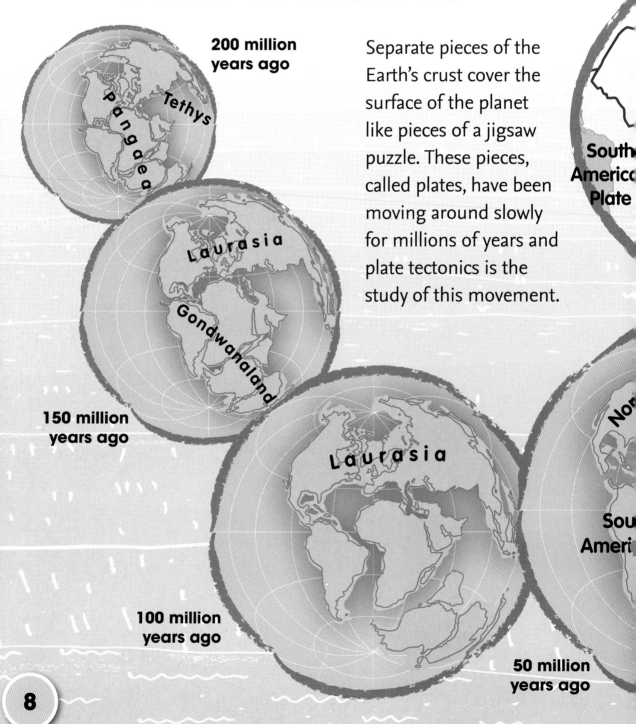

200 million years ago

Pangaea

Tethys

150 million years ago

Laurasia

Gondwanaland

100 million years ago

Laurasia

50 million years ago

South America Plate

Nor

Sou Ameri

Separate pieces of the Earth's crust cover the surface of the planet like pieces of a jigsaw puzzle. These pieces, called plates, have been moving around slowly for millions of years and plate tectonics is the study of this movement.

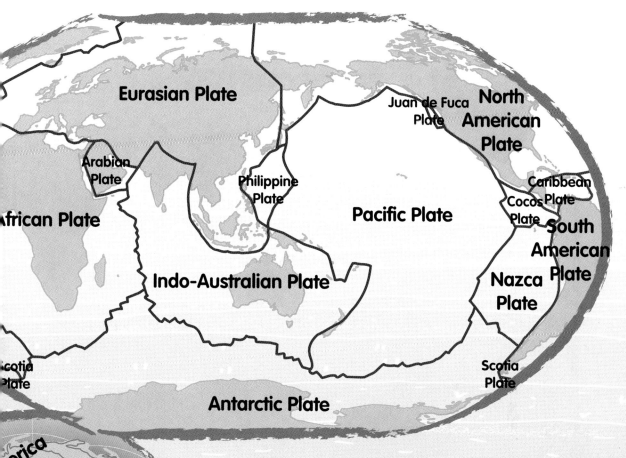

Eurasian Plate

Juan de Fuca Plate

North American Plate

Arabian Plate

Philippine Plate

Caribbean Plate

Cocos Plate

African Plate

Pacific Plate

South American Plate

Indo-Australian Plate

Nazca Plate

Scotia Plate

Scotia Plate

Antarctic Plate

America

Eurasia

Africa

Antarctica

Australia

About 200 million years ago – when dinosaurs lived – most land was joined together in an enormous landmass called Pangaea. Gradually the plates have drifted to make the shapes of the continents that we know today. Scientists know that areas of land that are now far apart were once joined together because they have found the same rocks and fossils on opposite sides of oceans.

Plate movement

Plates move very slowly, so slowly that we cannot feel it. They move at a speed of only a few centimetres every year – which is about the rate that our fingernails grow. Different plates move at different speeds and in different directions, and it is these movements that cause the

Conservative boundary

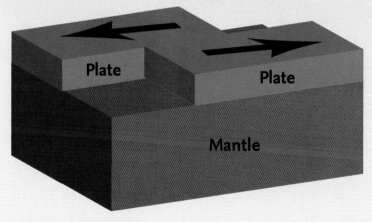

Conservative (or transform) boundaries lie on the edge of plates that are sliding or grinding sideways past each other. They stick together, then suddenly slip apart, causing an earthquake.

Constructive boundary

Constructive boundaries lie along the edges of plates that are moving away from each other. They are constr uctive because they build new areas of crust as magma comes up in the gaps between the plates and then cools to form new rocks.

violent activity of earthquakes and volcanoes. The areas where plates meet are called plate boundaries. There are three different kinds of boundary, depending on whether the plates on each side are sliding, colliding or pulling apart from each other.

Destructive boundary

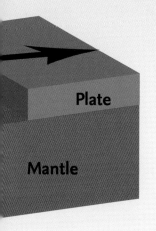

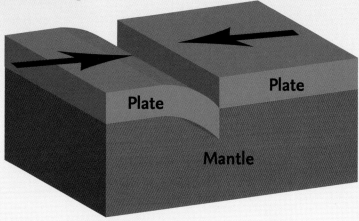

When plates are moving towards each other one of the plates pushes the other down into the mantle where part of it melts and is destroyed, so these are called destructive boundaries.

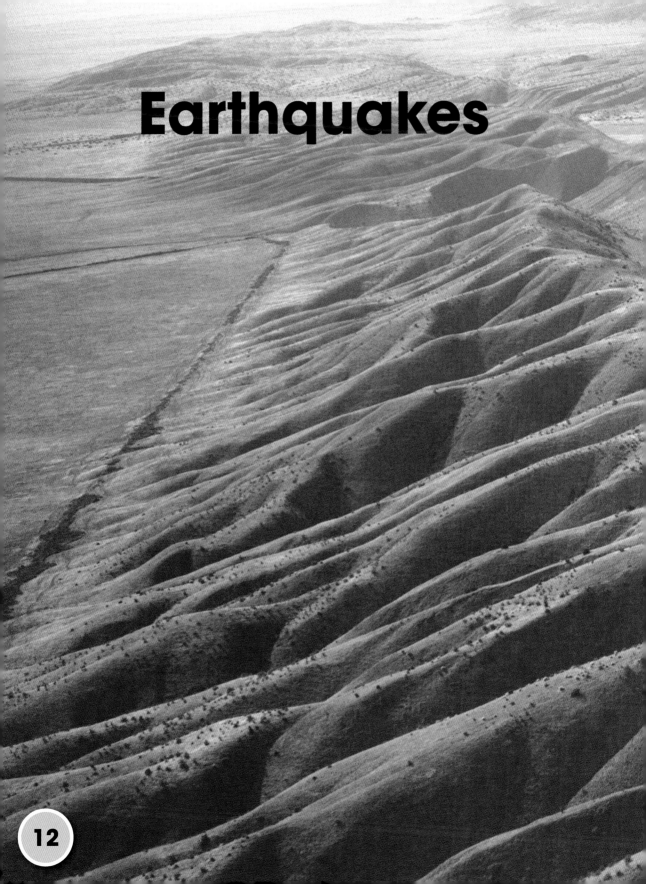

Earthquakes

What is an earthquake?

As the plates in the crust of the Earth move they develop cracks, or faults, where the rock is weak. When the edges of moving plates stick together they store up energy in the crust. An earthquake is a sudden release of this stored-up energy, mostly at weak places like faults along or near plate boundaries. Three main types of fault cause an earthquake – thrust, strike-slip and normal fault. Thrust faults often cause the most powerful earthquakes. All earthquakes have a central point on the Earth's surface, called the epicentre, and the waves of shaking, called seismic waves, which spread out from this centre can last between less than a second to a few minutes. Often there are aftershocks – small earthquakes that follow on after the main one – and these can last for weeks, months or even years.

Thrust fault

Most common at destructive plate boundaries

Block of rock
moves down

Block of rock
moves up

Strike-slip fault

Most common at conservative plate boundaries

Blocks of rock sliding
in opposite directions

Normal fault

Most common at constructive plate boundaries

Block of rock
moves up

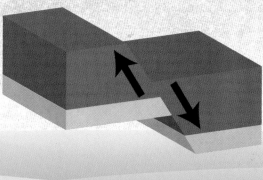

Block of rock
moves down

Measuring earthquakes

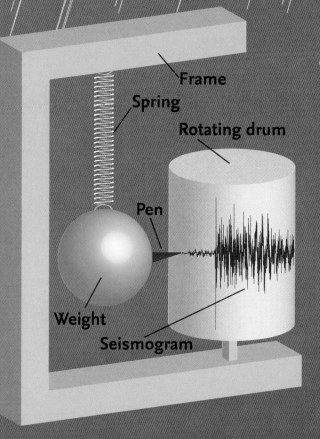

Frame

Spring

Rotating drum

Pen

Weight

Seismogram

Earthquake measurements are made using a seismograph. A heavy weight hangs on a spring and when the ground shakes the fixed frame of the seismograph shakes but the hanging weight does not. The seismograph records the difference in position between the shaking part of the seismograph and the part that does not move. Seismographs record movements on paper attached to a rotating drum although most modern instruments record their measurements using a computer. The graph of movements is called a seismogram. A pattern of big wiggles on a seismogram indicates a major earthquake.

Earthquake data is collected day and night, all round the world, and real-time seismograms of earthquakes are available to see on the internet at www.iris.edu/hq/ssn/schools/realtime

Scientists can measure earthquakes very accurately, and they know which areas are likely to have earthquakes in the future, but they cannot predict exactly when earthquakes will happen.

How often do earthquakes happen?

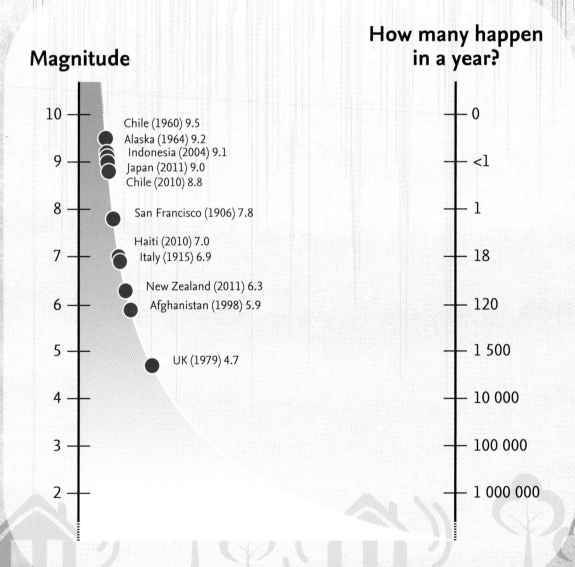

Magnitude

How many happen in a year?

Magnitude		How many in a year
10		0
	Chile (1960) 9.5	
	Alaska (1964) 9.2	
	Indonesia (2004) 9.1	
9	Japan (2011) 9.0	<1
	Chile (2010) 8.8	
8	San Francisco (1906) 7.8	1
	Haiti (2010) 7.0	
7	Italy (1915) 6.9	18
	New Zealand (2011) 6.3	
6	Afghanistan (1998) 5.9	120
5	UK (1979) 4.7	1 500
4		10 000
3		100 000
2		1 000 000

What does it feel like?

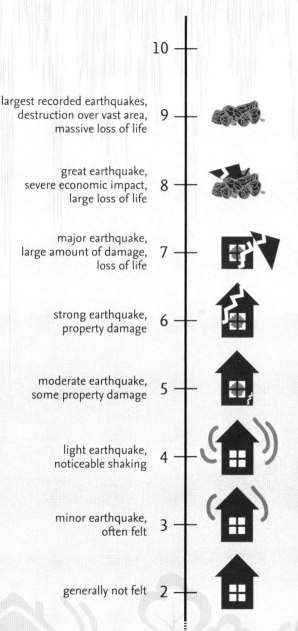

Magnitude	Description
10	
9	largest recorded earthquakes, destruction over vast area, massive loss of life
8	great earthquake, severe economic impact, large loss of life
7	major earthquake, large amount of damage, loss of life
6	strong earthquake, property damage
5	moderate earthquake, some property damage
4	light earthquake, noticeable shaking
3	minor earthquake, often felt
2	generally not felt

The size of an earthquake is measured on the moment magnitude scale. The larger the number, the bigger the earthquake. An earthquake of magnitude 3 is ten times more powerful than one of magnitude 2, and so on, so that an earthquake of magnitude 9 is ten million times more powerful than one of magnitude 2.

Small earthquakes are much more common than large ones. There are hundreds of earthquakes of less than magnitude 2 in the world every day, but the biggest earthquakes, with a magnitude over 8, are less frequent and happen only about once a year.

Where do earthquakes occur?

Earthquakes occur mainly at the boundaries of tectonic plates, where the plates slide under or over, or move alongside each other. A map of earthquake occurrences clearly shows the outline of the plates. The worst affected areas are China and Japan, southeast Asia, the western coasts of North and South America, and a zone across the Mediterranean, Middle East and central Asia.

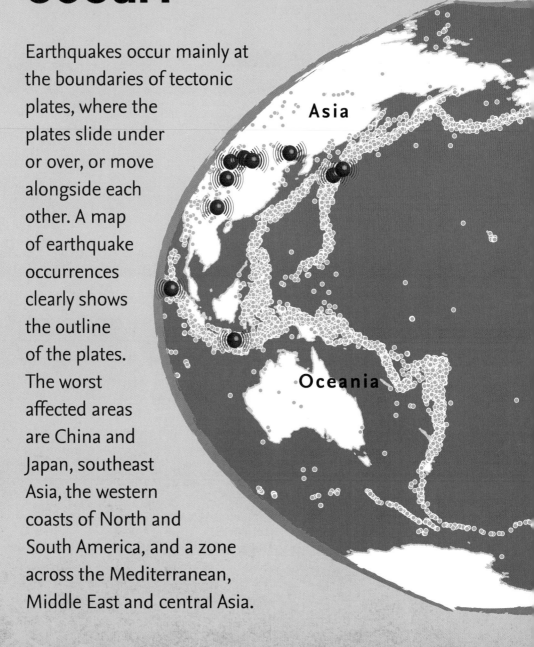

Asia

Oceania

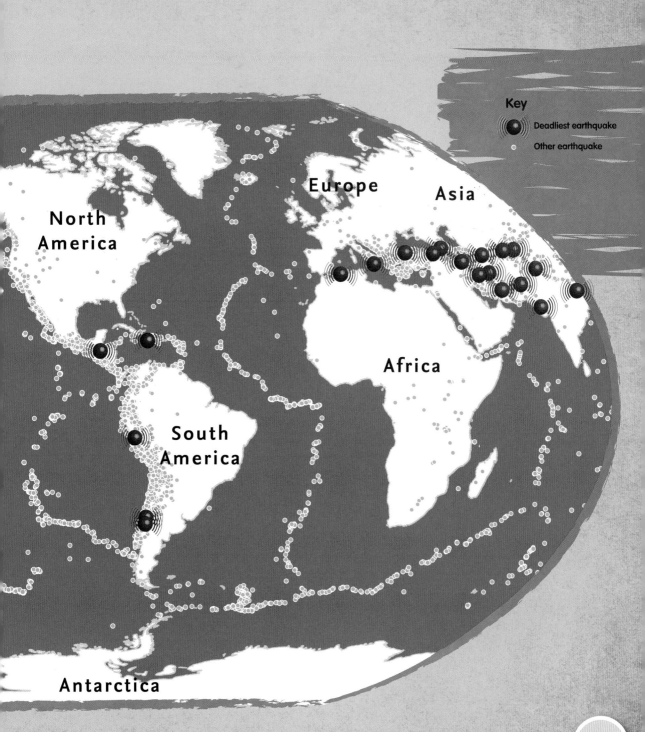

Key

Deadliest earthquake

Other earthquake

Europe

Asia

North
America

Africa

South
America

Antarctica

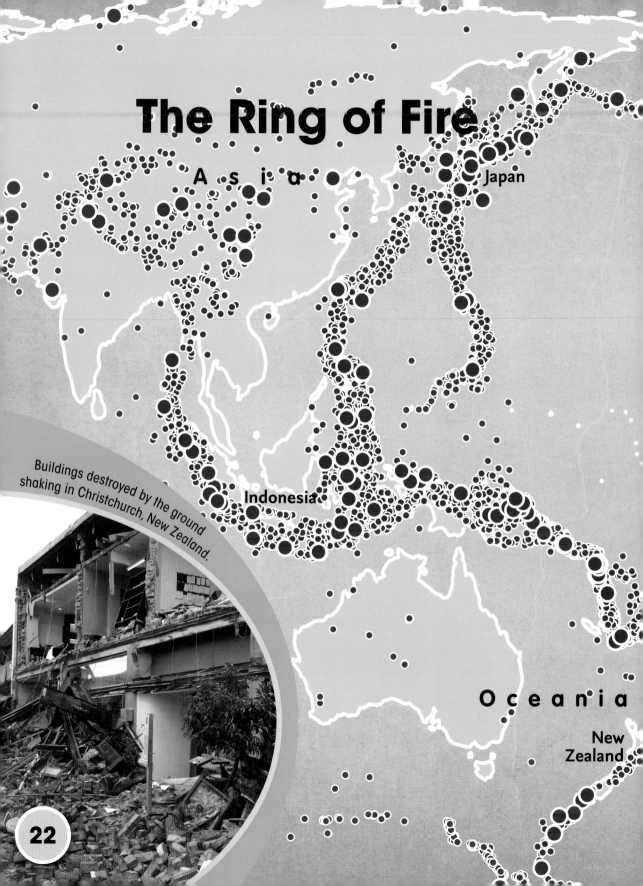

The Ring of Fire

A s i a

Japan

Indonesia

O c e a n i a

New
Zealand

Buildings destroyed by the ground
shaking in Christchurch, New Zealand.

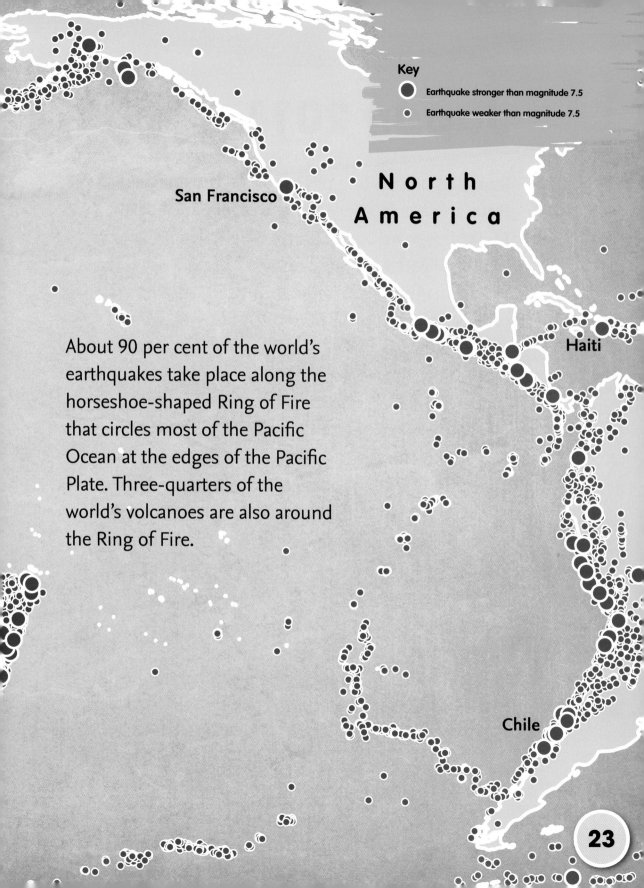

Key

● Earthquake stronger than magnitude 7.5

• Earthquake weaker than magnitude 7.5

San Francisco

**N o r t h
A m e r i c a**

Haiti

About 90 per cent of the world's earthquakes take place along the horseshoe-shaped Ring of Fire that circles most of the Pacific Ocean at the edges of the Pacific Plate. Three-quarters of the world's volcanoes are also around the Ring of Fire.

Chile

Japan 2011

Japan lies on the Ring of Fire, at the edge of the Pacific Plate, and it is in a very active area for earthquakes. Most houses are built to survive tremors and Japan is generally well prepared for small earthquakes. But the 9.0 magnitude earthquake that hit the east coast on the afternoon of 11 March 2011 was the largest recorded earthquake ever to hit the country. Scientists think that a 200 m section of rock in the Earth's crust suddenly uplifted, causing the earthquake and a huge tsunami that hit the coast, destroying towns and flooding the land.

- Over 10,000 people were killed and over half a million people lost their homes.
- Six million houses lost electricity and over one million people had no running water.
- A nuclear power station explosion caused by the earthquake forced thousands of people to evacuate their houses.

In the months after the disaster Japan had to rebuild houses, factories, roads, railways and ports.

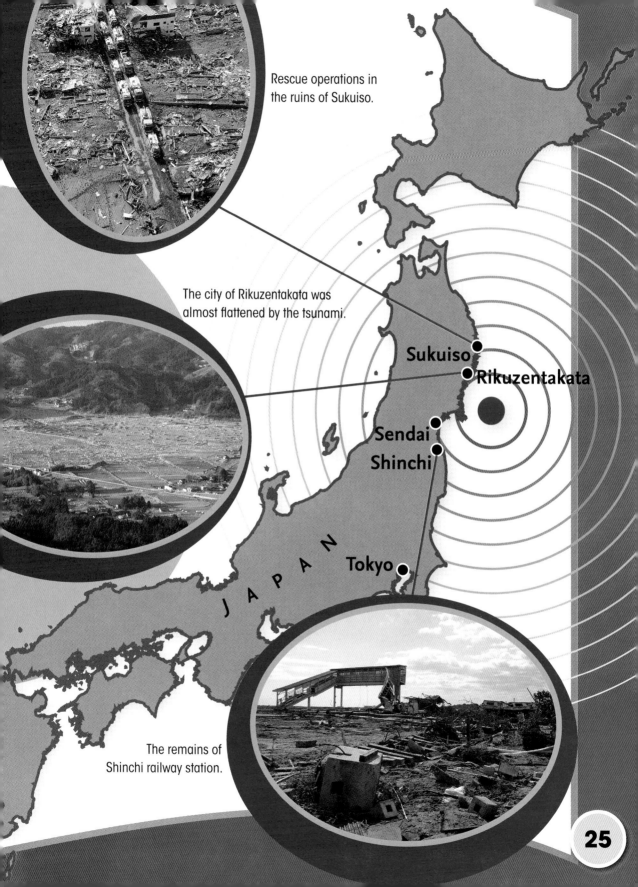

Rescue operations in the ruins of Sukuiso.

The city of Rikuzentakata was almost flattened by the tsunami.

Sukuiso

Rikuzentakata

Sendai

Shinchi

Tokyo

J A P A N

The remains of Shinchi railway station.

Deadliest earthquake

Chile suffers frequent earthquakes because it lies along the boundary of the South American Plate and the Nazca Plate. The earthquake that struck on the afternoon of 22 May 1960 measured 9.5, making it the most powerful earthquake ever measured in the world. It caused a tsunami that raced right across the Pacific Ocean, killing people in Hawaii, Japan and the Philippines.

The worst-affected city in Chile was Valdivia. Large areas were flooded from the tsunami and entire houses floated down the river. Estimates of the total number that died vary between about 2,000 and 6,000, and this number would have been much higher if it had been a more densely populated area.

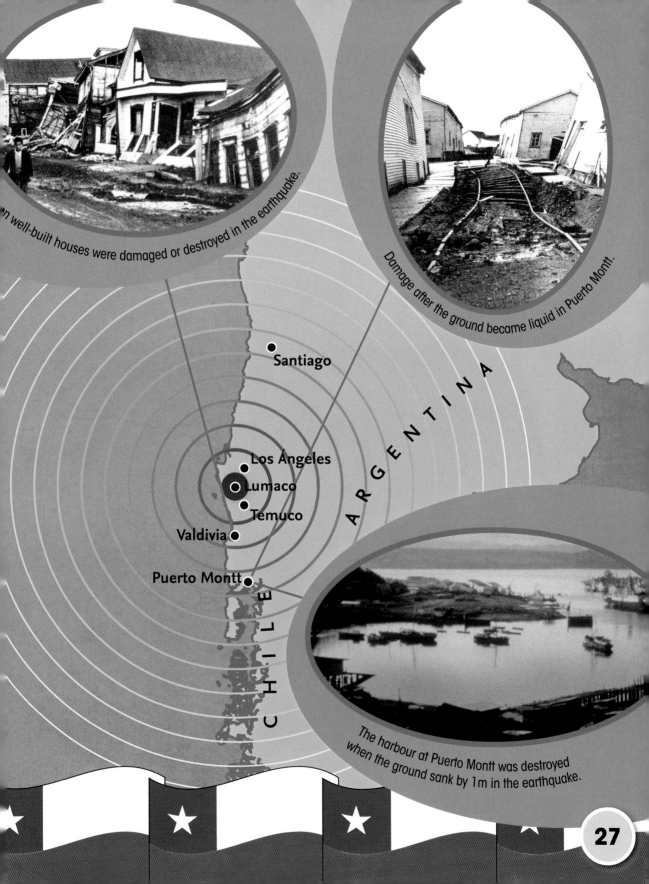

Well-built houses were damaged or destroyed in the earthquake.

Damage after the ground became liquid in Puerto Montt.

Santiago

Los Ángeles

Lumaco

Temuco

Valdivia

Puerto Montt

A R G E N T I N A

C H I L E

The harbour at Puerto Montt was destroyed when the ground sank by 1m in the earthquake.

San Francisco 1906

San Francisco sits on the San Andreas Fault, a major fault line that runs through California in the USA. Early in the morning of 18 April 1906 over 400 km of the fault line ruptured, violently shaking San Francisco and destroying half of the city. Buildings toppled and streets crumpled. Burst gas pipes and fallen stoves caused fires that spread furiously across the city. More people died from these fires than from the magnitude 7.7 earthquake itself. After the earthquake people thought carefully about how to rebuild the city to make it safer, if – or when – a major earthquake struck again.

The 1906 San Francisco earthquake was important in developing scientific understanding of why earthquakes happen, and it was also the first major earthquake for which the damage could be recorded by photography.

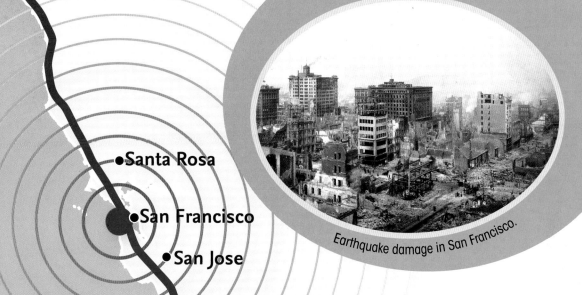
Earthquake damage in San Francisco.

●Santa Rosa

●San Francisco

●San Jose

UNITED STATES
OF AMERICA

San Andreas Fault

Many people were forced to leave their homes and live in temporary camps.

●Los Angeles

Fires burning after the earthquake.

29

Tsunamis

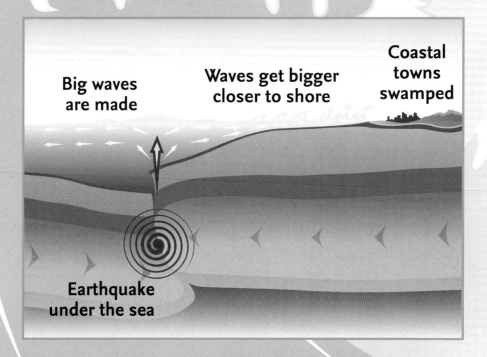

Big waves are made

Waves get bigger closer to shore

Coastal towns swamped

Earthquake under the sea

Look at a map showing earthquakes around the world and you will notice that many are under the sea. Water does not stop the tremors of an earthquake – instead it swells up into waves called tsunamis. These waves travel across the ocean reaching speeds up to 800 km per hour. Some tsunamis are just a few centimetres high but others are huge – up to about 30 m, which is five times as high as a house. When they hit a coast they can cause devastation, destroying beaches, crushing buildings and flooding towns.

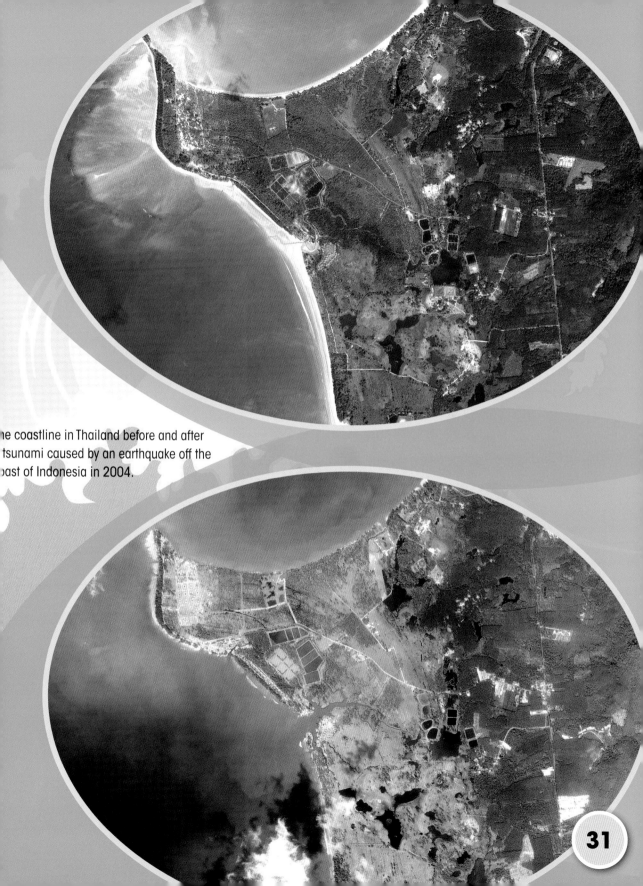

...he coastline in Thailand before and after ...tsunami caused by an earthquake off the ...oast of Indonesia in 2004.

Recent major earthquakes

Between 2001 and 2011, more than 18,500 earthquakes between magnitudes 5 and 9.3 were recorded. The list on the right shows some recent earthquakes and some of their effects. Earthquakes near populated areas are often most devastating because more people are affected, even if they are not of the highest magnitude.

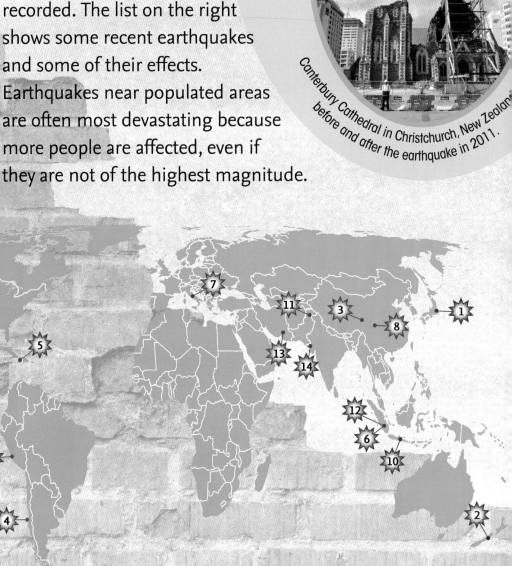

Canterbury Cathedral in Christchurch, New Zealand before and after the earthquake in 2011.

	Event	Mag.	Destruction
1	Japan March 2011	9.0	More than 10,000 killed; 17,000 reported missing; 125,000 buildings damaged; More than 500,000 homeless
2	Christchurch, NZ February 2011	6.3	More than 180 killed; 80% of water and sewer system damaged
3	Yushu, China April 2010	6.9	2,698 killed; 12,000 injured; 85% of buildings (11 schools) destroyed
4	Maule, Chile February 2010	8.8	521 killed; 370,000 homes damaged
5	Port-au-Prince, Haiti January 2010	7.0	Estimated 220,000 killed; 1,000,000 homeless
6	Sumatra, Indonesia December 2009	7.5	1,115 killed; 200,000 homes damaged
7	Abruzzo, Italy April 2009	6.3	308 killed; 1,500 injured; 3,000 – 11,000 buildings damaged; 65,000 homeless
8	Sichuan, China May 2008	7.9	69,000 killed; 5,000,000 homeless
9	Chincha Alta, Peru August 2007	8.0	519 killed; 85% of buildings destroyed in Pisco and Chincha Alta; Many homeless
10	Java, Indonesia May 2006	6.3	5,782 killed; 36,299 injured; 135,000 homes damaged; 1,500,000 homeless
11	Pakistan October 2005	7.6	80,000 killed; 32,000 buildings collapsed
12	Sumatra, Indonesia December 2004	9.1	230,000 killed in 12 countries; 1,300,000 affected; widespread water and food shortages
13	Southeastern Iran December 2003	6.6	26,000 killed; 30,000 injured; 85% of buildings destroyed in the Nahrin area; 100,000 homeless
14	India January 2001	7.7	20,000 killed; 167,000 injured; 600,000 homeless

Human impacts

Whole cities can be destroyed in minutes by the violent shaking of an earthquake. Immediately after an earthquake efforts need to concentrate on the rescue of people that might still be in the rubble, and the provision of basic necessities such as water, food, clothing, shelter and medical supplies for those who have survived. Often it is necessary to rely on rescue teams and aid from other countries because local emergency services have been destroyed. Long-term recovery can take many years. In the weeks, months and years that follow it is necessary to rebuild and also look for ways to be more prepared if an earthquake strikes again.

Short term effects of an earthquake

- Burst gas and water pipes, and damaged electricity wires increase the risk of fire and flooding.
- There are many injured people at a time when hospitals might have been destroyed or be without medical staff.
- No clean drinking water, food supplies or clothes, so help must be provided from other areas to reduce the risk of starvation or disease.
- Homes are destroyed so temporary shelters must be provided.
- Roads, bridges, ports and airports are destroyed so it is difficult to send help where it is needed – helicopters are often used.

Long term effects of an earthquake

- Cost of rebuilding homes, schools, hospitals, offices, airports, roads, and railways. Even standing buildings may be unstable and need rebuilding.
- Distress of losing relatives and friends – and there may be many children or old people without anyone to look after them.
- Jobs are lost in shops, offices and factories, and it can take a long time to build businesses back up again.
- There might always be the worry of when the next earthquake might be.

A huge number of buildings were completetly destroyed in Port-au-Prince, Haiti, on 12 January 2010. Many of the victims made their home in a big tent city.

Earthquake facts

 1 The **largest recorded earthquake** in the world was a magnitude 9.5 that hit Chile in May 1960. The seismic waves shook the entire Earth for several days.

 2 The **earthquake with the highest death toll** was in 1556 in central China. It struck a region where most people lived in caves carved from soft rock. These dwellings collapsed during the earthquake, killing an estimated 830,000 people.

 3 The **earliest recorded evidence of an earthquake** has been traced back to 1831 BC in eastern China.

 4 At 609 km below the ocean floor, a magnitude 8.3 earthquake on Russia's Kamchatka Peninsula in May 2013 is believed to be the **deepest-ever recorded earthquake**. Most earthquakes start less than 80 km below the surface.

5 The 2004 Sumatra earthquake was the **longest-lasting earthquake** ever recorded. Small earthquakes last less than a second, most larger ones a few seconds or a few minutes – but this one carried on shaking for 10 minutes.

6 The **longest-ever earthquake survivor** was 40 year-old Naqsha Bibi who survived in a crouched position trapped in the kitchen of her collapsed house for 63 days after a 2004 earthquake in Pakistan. She survived by eating rotting food and drinking water that trickled through the house.

7 The **largest-ever recorded tsunami** was in Lituya Bay, Alaska, USA in July 1958. An earthquake caused a rockslide, which set in motion a staggeringly high 524 m wave that swept away millions of trees on its way to the Gulf of Alaska.

8 With estimates of between $200 and $300 billion to repair and compensate for damage, the 2011 earthquake and tsunami in Japan is the world's **most expensive earthquake** on record.

Volcanoes

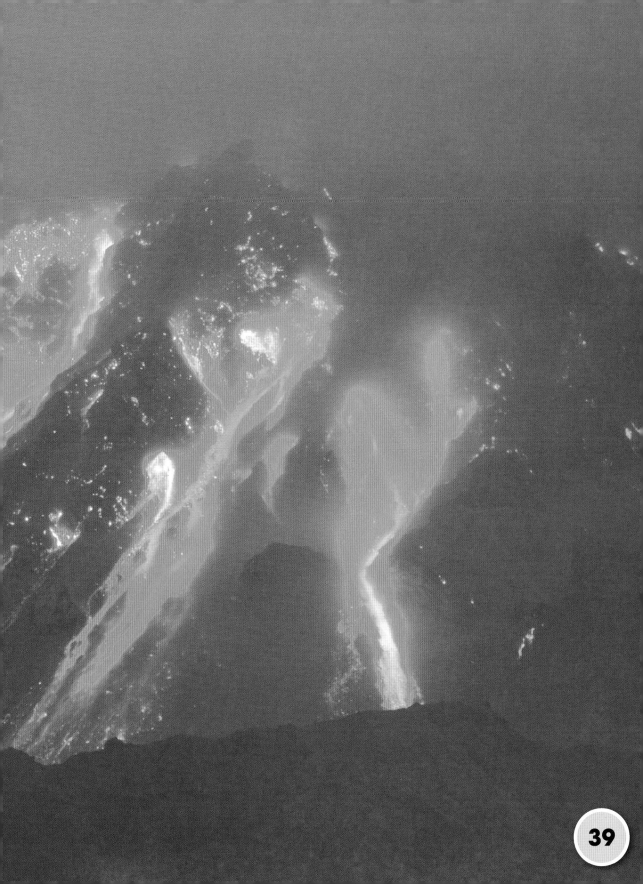

What is a volcano?

The word volcano originally comes from the name of the Roman god of fire, Vulcan. He was blacksmith to the gods, making their weapons from hot metal.

Volcanoes form where red-hot, liquid rock called magma is under pressure beneath the Earth's crust. It finds the weakest place it can, and bursts up through a crack or hole in the Earth's surface. Magma rises up from a storage chamber called the magma chamber, which is deep underground, and it pours out on to the Earth's surface through outlets called vents. The main vent is the main route for magma to escape, but sometimes magma is forced out of smaller outlets called secondary vents that lead off from the main vent. Over time, with several eruptions, the build up of lava, ash and dust forms the cone shape characteristic of many volcanoes.

Magma is called lava once it has come to the surface of the Earth. Sometimes the magma spills out gradually and lava creeps along slower than the speed we walk. More deadly are pyroclastic flows – they are mixtures of hot steam, ash and rock that roll down a

Inside a volcano

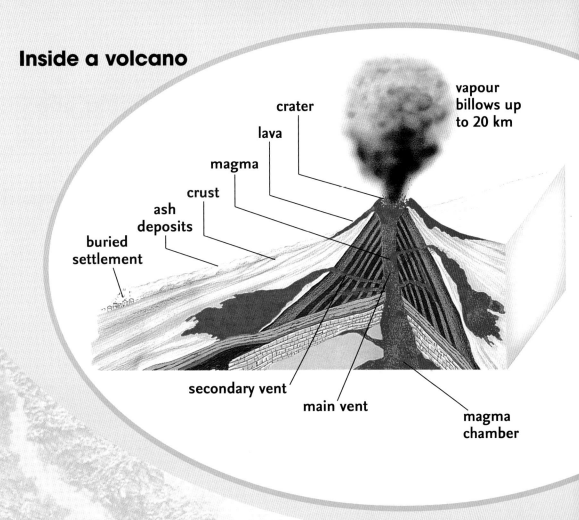

vapour billows up to 20 km

crater

lava

magma

crust

ash deposits

buried settlement

secondary vent

main vent

magma chamber

volcano during an eruption, burning and flattening everything they reach. They move at speeds faster than a jet plane – much faster than anyone could run to escape. If the magma gets blocked on its way out it may burst out in a violent eruption with clouds of ash and dust, often releasing poisonous gases like hydrogen sulphide.

Types of volcanoes

Volcanoes can be many different shapes and sizes. Most are cone-shaped mountains or hills, built up from cooled lava and ash from several eruptions over thousands or millions of years. Some volcanoes do not look like mountains at all, but are long cracks in the Earth's surface where lava escapes.

Active volcanoes could erupt at any time, although scientists can usually predict when eruptions are most likely. Dormant volcanoes are 'sleeping' – they are not active, but they might still erupt again one day. Extinct volcanoes are ones that have not erupted for over 10,000 years. Scientists think that these very old volcanoes are unlikely to erupt again but of course nobody can ever be completely certain.

Anak Krakatau, Indonesia – an active volcano erupting.

Fissure volcano

This is when magma erupts from a long crack in the Earth's surface, often where two of the Earth's plates are pulling apart from each other.

Shield volcano

A shield volcano is low and wide. Its sides are gently sloping and sometimes it is not obvious that it is a volcano at all. It has formed from thin, runny flowing lava that has cooled slowly.

Dome volcano

Dome volcanoes have steep, convex slopes that form when thick lava cools quickly.

Ash-cinder volcano

These volcanoes have cones made of alternate layers of ash and cinder.

Composite volcano

A composite volcano has a steep cone shape built up of layers of erupted ash and lava.

Caldera volcano

These are old volcanoes with large, collapsed craters, often with small new craters inside them.

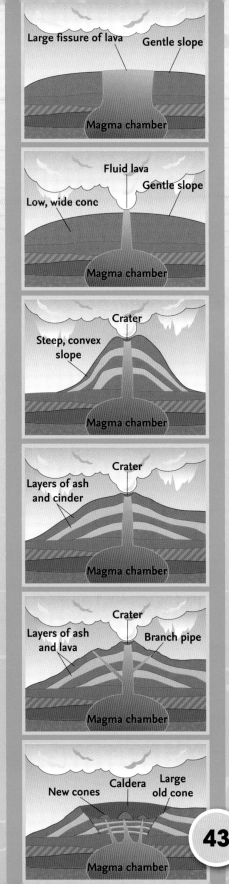

Supervolcanoes

Supervolcanoes are massive volcanoes that produce the largest eruptions of all. They produce about a thousand times more lava than an average large volcano. Eruptions are very rare, happening hundreds of thousands of years apart. The last one was 74,000 years ago, and we do not know where, or when, the next one will be. It might not be for another million years – or it might be much sooner.

Supervolcanoes erupt over volcanic hotspots, which are weak places on the Earth's crust where magma can rise and burst to the surface.

Old Faithful geyser, Yellowstone, USA

A beautiful geyser landscape at Yellowstone, USA.

Their explosive eruptions leave vast shallow craters in the Earth's surface called calderas, and these are the site of some amazing volcanic features such as geysers and bubbling mud pools. Geysers form when hot rock below the surface heats up water in an underground chamber — when the water boils it pushes up and spurts out in a fountain above the surface.

Yellowstone National Park in the USA is the most famous example of a supervolcano. It lies in the ancient caldera of several giant eruptions between 640,000 and 2 million years ago. If, or when, it erupts again it would have worldwide catastrophic effects. About half of the world's geysers are at Yellowstone, making it a very popular place for tourists to visit.

Effects of volcanic eruptions

Volcanic eruptions can have a devastating effect on people and the environment but some people choose to live near volcanoes, perhaps because it is their home, but also because volcanoes can bring benefits as well as dangers.

Eyjafjallajökull erupting in Iceland on 12 May 2010. The eruption created an ash cloud over northern Europe that caused enormous disruption to air travel.

Positive and negative effects of an eruption

Negative

- Fast-moving lava and mudflows can destroy settlements and kill people.
- Ash can fall over a large area, choking people and animals, and covering vegetation and crops.
- Beautiful natural landscapes can be destroyed.
- There is always the worry of when the next eruption might be.

Positive

- Amazing new landscapes are created, with dramatic lava formations that can attract tourists.
- Lava and fallen ash eventually breaks down to make a fertile soil, rich in nutrients that are good for farming.
- The heat under the ground in a volcanic area can be used to create geothermal energy, which is used to heat homes and make electricity.

Tourists relaxing in the famous Blue Lagoon. This geothermal spa is one of the most visited attractions in Iceland.

Where do volcanoes occur?

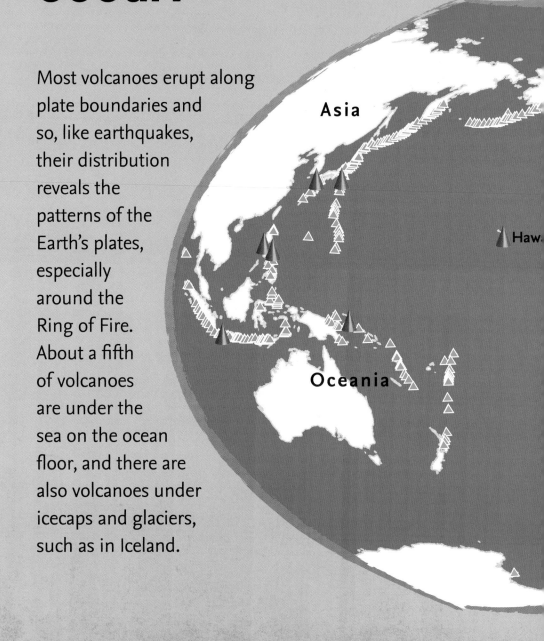

Most volcanoes erupt along plate boundaries and so, like earthquakes, their distribution reveals the patterns of the Earth's plates, especially around the Ring of Fire. About a fifth of volcanoes are under the sea on the ocean floor, and there are also volcanoes under icecaps and glaciers, such as in Iceland.

Asia

Haw[a]

Oceania

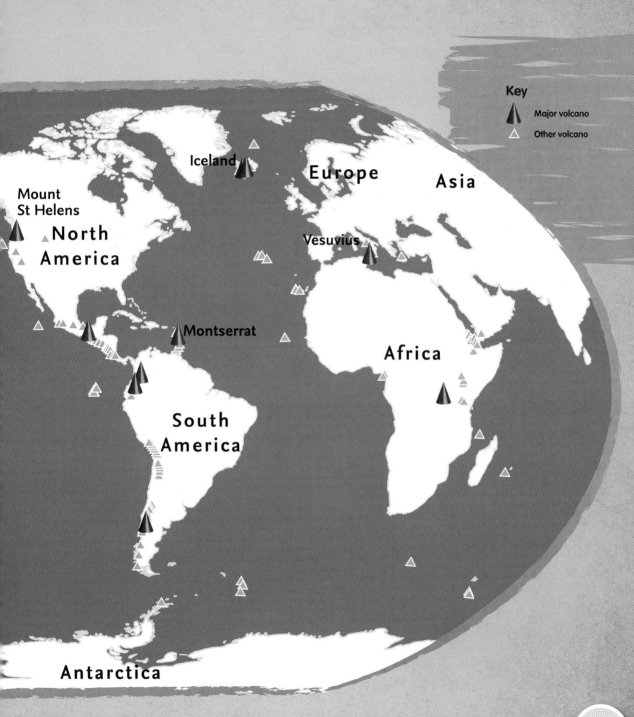

Key

🌋 Major volcano

△ Other volcano

Iceland

Europe

Asia

Mount
St Helens

North
America

Vesuvius

Montserrat

Africa

South
America

Antarctica

Montserrat

Montserrat is a small and beautiful tropical island in the Caribbean. It is about 16 km long and 11 km wide. In the southern part of the island is a volcanic area called Soufrière Hills.

In 1995, after being dormant for 300 years, a volcano in the Soufrière Hills began erupting. At first there were warning signs with small earthquakes and little eruptions of dust – then eruptions became bigger. For the next five years the volcano continued to be very active, sometimes spewing out lava and sometimes spitting out steam and ash. The worst eruptions were in 1997 when the southern part of the island was devastated by pyroclastic flows. Over half of the island was covered with volcanic ash, and ash even fell on neighbouring islands 40 km away.

Montserrat after the eruptions

Key
- • Resettlement area
- Safe area
- Risky area
- Dangerous area
- Area covered with volcanic ash
- → Lava flows between 1995 and 1999
- ✳ Main volcanic eruptions from 1995
- Capital city destroyed
- ✳ Airport destroyed
- ✕ Port destroyed

Little Bay Lookout
St John's
St Peter's
Plymouth
Soufrière Hills

The top of a church in Plymouth, which was buried under several metres of volcanic ash and mud in 1997.

Effects of the eruptions

- About twenty settlements were badly damaged by lava flows, including the capital city, Plymouth, which was completely destroyed.
- People had to be evacuated to safety and over three-quarters of the islanders left Montserrat. By 2011 many had come back, but the population was still less than half of what it was before the eruptions.
- Nineteen people were killed – they had wanted to stay to look after their farms, and they left it too late to leave.
- The airport was completely destroyed and a new airport had to be built in the north of the island. The only hospital and many roads were also destroyed.
- Fewer tourists visited although when the eruptions calmed down people became interested in seeing the volcano, so now there are more visitors again.

Mount St Helens

When Mount St Helens in the USA erupted on 18 May 1980 it completely blew the top off the volcano. A cloud of ash blasted up over 20 km high in one of the most explosive eruptions ever recorded. Massive mudflows of stones, ash and water poured down the mountainside and millions of trees were flattened. Before the eruption the side of the volcano had bulged outwards where the magma was building up, so an eruption was expected, but nobody had realised how enormous it would be. Over 50 people were killed, mainly forestry workers and tourists, because they thought they were a safe distance away from any danger.

Ashfall across the USA after the eruption

The spectacular eruption lasted for nine hours and created plumes of ash that fell in a wide area across the country. Roads were closed and air travel was disrupted because of poor visibility.

Spokane
Ritzville
Yakima
Mount
St Helens

UNITED STATES OF AMERICA

Key
5 cm to 12 cm
1 cm to 5 cm
Up to 1 cm

The eruption left a gaping crater in the side of Mount St Helens, totally changing the surrounding landscape.

Kauai ▲

Hot spot volcanoes: Hawaii

▲ Oahu

Hot spots are places where especially hot magma is pushed up to the Earth's surface. The magma burns through at weak places on the Earth's crust that are not necessarily on plate boundaries. The Hawaiian Islands, in the Pacific Ocean, are the most famous examples of hot spot volcanoes. They formed when a volcano grew over a hotspot, then as the plate moved on, another volcano formed. In this way, a chain of volcanoes was created.

The island of Hawaii is the largest and youngest volcanic island in a chain of islands that began to form over a million years ago. It has several major volcanoes, including Mauna Loa, the largest volcano in the world by volume. Southeast of Hawaii is the undersea volcano of Loihi – it is still about 975 m below the surface of the ocean but in thousands of years if it erupts above sea level it will be the newest island in the chain.

Creation of the Hawaiian islands by hot spot volcanoes.

Koko Head Volcano, Oahu.

Maui

▲

Mauna Kea
▲

Hawaii

▲
Mauna
Loa

Kilauea
▲

Historic eruptions: Vesuvius

Mount Vesuvius, in Italy, is the only active volcano in mainland Europe and its eruption in AD 79 is one of the most famous in history. Before then it had not erupted for 800 years. During the violent eruption a deadly cloud of poisonous gas, stones, ash and fumes rose up 33 km into the air. An estimated 16,000 people died, and the Roman cities of Pompeii and Herculaneum were completely buried in ash. Most of the people who died were killed by the hot ash, which made them choke so they could not breathe.

Vesuvius is so famous partly because it was the first ever eruption to be described in detail and partly because of the archaeological excavations at Pompeii and Herculaneum.

Mount Vesuvius towering over the modern city of Naples in Italy.

Plaster casts of Pompeii victims.

I T A L Y

Naples
● ▲ **Vesuvius**

There was hardly any time to escape so people died as they ran through the streets or hid in houses. Archaeologists uncovered many body-shaped cavities of people. These cavities were filled with plaster to show the exact position the person was in when they died.

Volcanic rocks

As lava cools above ground it hardens to form igneous rocks. Aa is thick lava that flows slowly, cooling to make a rough-surfaced rock. Runny fast-flowing lava is called pahoehoe and that cools to look like smooth coils of rope. Pillow lava forms when volcanoes erupt underwater or lava flows into the sea. These rounded lumps of lava look like pillows piled on top of each other.

Pillow lava near Oamaru, New Zealand.

Aa lava and pahoehoe lava, Hawaii.

Basalt is a common type of lava that has cooled slowly, forming large, straight-sided columns of rock. These rocks are strong and make good building materials.

Pumice is formed from lava full of gas bubbles that has cooled quickly. It is one of the very few rocks that can float in water.

Pumice

Basalt columns in Boyabat, Turkey.

Basalt columns of the Giant's Causeway, Northern Ireland.

Volcanoes on other planets and moons

The Earth is not the only volcanic planet in the Solar System. With over a thousand volcanoes, the neighbouring planet of Venus has the most volcanic features, but all of them are probably extinct.

The largest volcano in the Solar System is also not on Earth, but on Earth's other neighbouring planet of Mars. Olympus Mons is a giant shield volcano that rises to a height of 24 km and measures an amazing 600 km wide.

Io, one of the moons of Jupiter, has over 400 active volcanoes, making it the most geologically active object in the Solar System. The volcanic flows on its surface make it a very colourful moon.

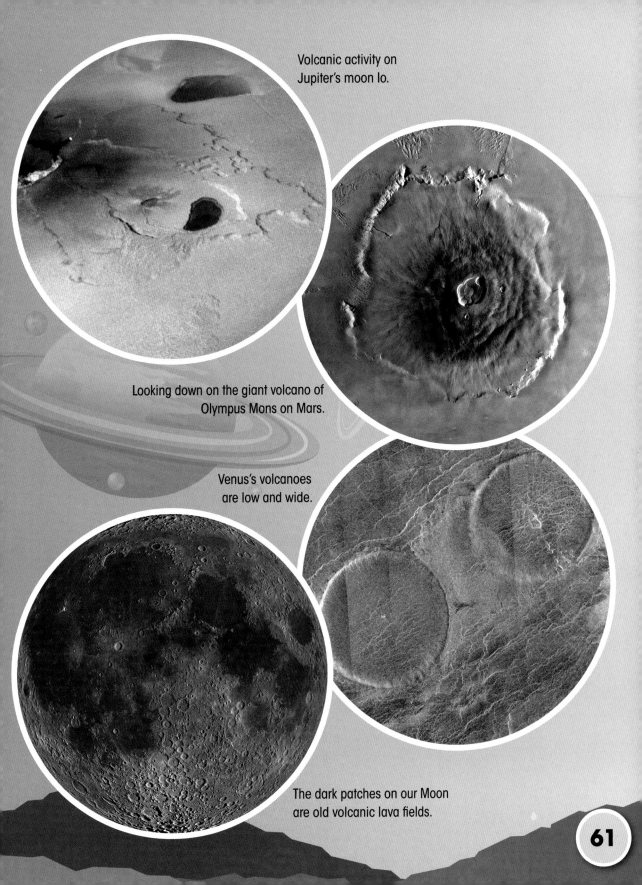

Volcanic activity on
Jupiter's moon Io.

Looking down on the giant volcano of
Olympus Mons on Mars.

Venus's volcanoes
are low and wide.

The dark patches on our Moon
are old volcanic lava fields.

Volcanic landscapes

Most news coverage focuses on the destruction wreaked by volcanoes but over time volcanic eruptions also create landscapes that people have lived in and benefitted from for thousands of years. Volcanic rocks provide building materials, and the heat from volcanoes is used in some countries to generate electricity.

Volcanoes add nutrients to the soil, creating perfect fertile conditions for crops to grow in. Ash is very fine and breaks down quickly to mix in with the soil. In many places people farm the lower slopes of volcanoes, such as in Indonesia, Japan, Hawaii, the Philippines and Italy. In some places the soil would otherwise be very poor and thin so volcanic soils mean that crops like vines, fruit and vegetables can be grown which otherwise would not be possible.

Other volcanic slopes are too steep for farming but instead provide safe places for rare plants to grow and animals to live.

Fern growing in lava on Hawaii.
Moss growing on volcanic rocks in Iceland.
Vineyard in volcanic soil on Lanzarote.
Grapes growing in Lanzarote.
A landscape of lush vegetation in Hawaii.

Volcano facts

1 At 6,893 m high, the **highest volcano** in the world is Ojos del Selado on the border between Argentina and Chile in the Andes mountains. However, if measured from the seafloor to include the height under the sea as well as above sea level, then the dormant volcano of Mauna Kea in Hawaii is about 10.2 km (10,200 m) high, making it not only the highest volcano in the world but also the highest mountain in the world.

2 The **largest volcano** in the world in terms of volume and area covered is the giant shield volcano of Mauna Loa on Hawaii. Its dome is 120 km long and over 100 km wide.

3 The Waimangu Geyser, near Rotorua in New Zealand, was the **most powerful geyser in the world.** Spectacular eruptions of black mud and rock were observed up to 460 m high, although the geyser only lasted between 1900 and 1904.

4 The **longest-lasting eruption** is the volcanic island of Stromboli in Italy – it has been erupting almost continuously for over 2,000 years.

5 The **tallest currently active geyser** is the Steamboat Geyser in Yellowstone National Park, USA, which reaches a maximum height of 130 m.

6 In 1963 an undersea volcano created the **newest land mass** on Earth, Surtsey, an island that lies off the southwest coast of Iceland. It is named after Surt, a fire giant from Norse mythology.

7 The **deadliest eruptions in recorded history** were from the fissures at Laki, south Iceland between 1783 and 1784. Poisonous gases caused the deaths of animals and made crops fail, with global consequences leading to the death of an estimated 6 million people.

8 The **loudest volcanic eruption** was the explosion of Krakatoa, Indonesia in 1883 – it was heard over 3,500 km away and is believed to be the loudest sound ever heard in recorded history.

Crossword

ACROSS

2   Volcano which destroyed Pompeii (8)

4   A volcano which could erupt (6)

7   Light, holey volcanic rock (6)

8   Volcano – Mount St _____ (6)

9   Molten rock on Earth's surface (4)

11   When the ground shakes (10)

14   The very centre of Earth (4)

17   Where hotspot volcanoes are found (6)

18   Moving piece of Earth's crust (5)

19   Giant wave caused by earthquake (7)

21   Scientific word for plate movement (8)

23   Island where Plymouth was destroyed (10)

25   A sleeping volcano (7)

26   A word to describe volcanic soil (7)

27   Not solid or liquid (3)

28   How often an earthquake occurs (9)

29   Fast moving, hot ash and rock flows (11)

30   Fine, grey dust from volcanoes (3)

DOWN

1   Pacific country where there was an earthquake and tsunami in 2011 (5)

3   Town on the San Andreas Fault (3,9)

5   Mountain made by eruption and lava (7)

6   Superheated water spout (6)

10   The layer of molten rock inside Earth (6)

12   Where blocks of rock in the Earth's plates slide past each other (5)

13   Numeric description of how violent an earthquake was (9)

14   Thin outermost layer of the planet (5)

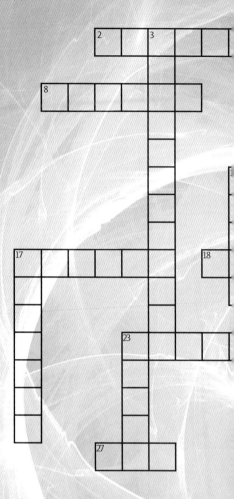

15   Island in the Caribbean where an earthquake caused devastation in 2010 (5)

16   Earthquakes can cause buildings to catch _____ (4)

17   Hawaii is an example of this kind of volcano (7)

20   Instrument used to record earthquakes (11)

22   South American country where big earthquakes have happened (5)

23   What lava is called when it's still under the surface (5)

24   A volcano which doesn't erupt any more (7)

Useful words

aa	Lava with a rough surface when it hardens.
active volcano	A volcano that might still erupt, even if it has not erupted recently.
aftershock	Small shocks that follow after the main shockwaves of an earthquake.
ash	Very fine particles of rock blown from an erupting volcano.
basalt	A dark-coloured volcanic rock formed from slowly-cooled lava.
cinder	Magma that has erupted from a volcano then cooled into pebble-sized pieces before falling to the ground.
caldera	A large, shallow crater usually formed by the collapse of a volcanic cone into a vent.
conservative plate boundary	The boundary of two plates that are sliding or grinding sideways past each other.
constructive plate boundary	The boundary of two plates moving away from each other.
core	The central part of the Earth made of a molten outer core and a solid inner core.
crater	A hollow created when an eruption blows the top off the volcano.
crust	The rocky 'skin' of the Earth's surface.
destructive plate boundary	The boundary of two plates moving towards each other.
dormant volcano	A volcano that has not erupted for thousands of years, but could still become active.
earthquake	Shaking of the ground caused by movements of the Earth's crust.
epicentre	The point on the Earth's surface exactly above the centre of an earthquake.
eruption	The forcing of solids, liquids or gases onto the Earth's surface by volcanic activity.
extinct volcano	A volcano that has not erupted for thousands of years and is unlikely to erupt again.
fault	A large crack in the Earth's crust where blocks of rock slide past each other.
geothermal energy	Energy that comes from deep underground heat.

geyser	An ejection of boiling water and steam that surfaces at intervals from a hole in the Earth's crust.
hydrogen sulphide	One of the poisonous gases produced in a volcanic eruption.
igneous rock	Rocks formed by the cooling of magma below ground or as cooled lava above ground.
lava	Magma that has reached the Earth's surface.
magma	Hot, liquid rock from beneath the Earth's surface.
magma chamber	The storage area for hot, liquid rock below the surface of a volcano.
main vent	The largest outlet for magma to escape to the surface in a volcano – it leads from the magma chamber to the Earth's surface.
mantle	The rocky part of the Earth between the crust and the core.
molten	Melted by heat.
pahoehoe	Smooth-surfaced lava that looks like coils of rope when it hardens.
pillow lava	Lava that has erupted under water and cooled to form pillow shapes.
plates	Separate pieces of the Earth's crust.
plate tectonics	The study of the movement of pieces of the Earth's crust.
pumice	Light-coloured volcanic rock formed by the expansion of gas in erupting lava.
pyroclastic flow	A hot mixture of steam, ash and rock that rolls down a volcano at great speed during an eruption.
secondary vent	A small outlet for magma to escape that leads off the main vent of a volcano.
seismic waves	Vibrations of the Earth during an earthquake.
seismograph	An instrument that measures the movement of the ground caused by earthquakes.
shield volcano	A low, flat volcano formed from runny lava that cooled slowly.
tsunami	A wave caused by a volcanic eruption or earthquake under the sea.
vent	The holes in a volcano out of which magma flows.

Index

Crossword answers

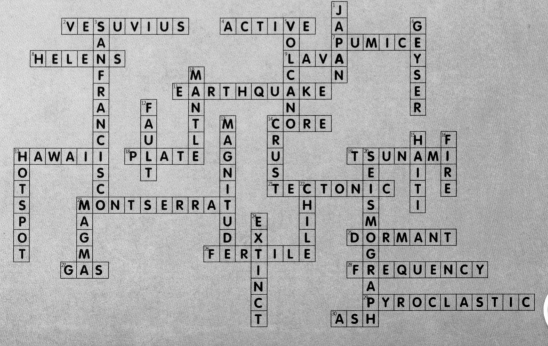

Acknowledgements

Image credits

Cover image: Ammit Jack/Shutterstock.com

2-3 Catmando/Shutterstock.com
4-5 seismograph © ermess/Shutterstock.com
volcano graphic © Matthew Cole/Shutterstock.com
volcano image © beboy/Shutterstock.com
6-7 landscapes © kstudija/Shutterstock.com
cut away globe © Webspark/Shutterstock.com
8-9 background © VOOK/Shutterstock.com
10-11 background © Swill Klitch/Shutterstock.com
12-13 San Andreas Fault Peter Menzel/Science Photo Library
14-15 background yellow © Polina Katritch/Shutterstock.com
background hills © Hermin/Shutterstock.com
buildings © Mike Elliott/Shutterstock.com
16-17 seismograph © ermess/Shutterstock.com
seismograph photo © Cico/Shutterstock.com
spring in seismograph diagram © Aleksangel/
Shutterstock.com
18-19 background yellow © Polina Katritch/Shutterstock.com
seismograph © ermess/Shutterstock.com
earthquake houses © Vaju Ariel/Shutterstock.com
rubble rocks © Lucy Ya/Shutterstock.com
20-21 background parchment © pashabo/Shutterstock.com
22-23 background parchment © pashabo/Shutterstock.com
earthquake photo © Darrenp/Shutterstock.com
24-25 pulse graphic © casejustin/Shutterstock.com
Fire Vehicles photo © Mass Communication Specialist
3rd Class
Dylan McCord/Wikipedia
Rikuzentakata image © Mitsukuni Sato/ Akira Kouchiyama/
Wikipedia
Shinchi image © Kuha455405/Wikipedia
26-27 pulse graphic © casejustin/Shutterstock.com
background parchment © pashabo/Shutterstock.com
Valdivia street © Pierre St. Amand/NOAA/Science
Photo Library
Puerto Montt rail line © Pierre St. Amand/NOAA/Science
Photo Library
Puerto Montt dock © Pierre St. Amand/NOAA/Science
Photo Library
28-29 background parchment © pashabo/Shutterstock.com
background fault line © Siianti/Shutterstock.com
pulse graphic © casejustin/Shutterstock.com
earthquake damage © National Archives and Records
Administration/Chadwick H. D/Wikipedia
displaced victims of the SF earthquake © unknown/
Wikipedia
mission district burning © National Archives and Records
Administration/Chadwick H. D/Wikipedia
30-31 wave background © Timmary/Shutterstock.com
tsunami diagram © daulon/Shutterstock.com
Thai coastline before tsunami © GeoEye/ Science Photo
Library
Thai coastline after tsunami © GeoEye/ Science Photo Library
32-33 Canterbury Cathedral © Graham Prentice/Shutterstock.com
ruins of the Anglican Cathedral © NigelSpiers/
Shutterstock.com
old brick wall © Martin Capek/Shutterstock.com
background yellow © Polina Katritch/Shutterstock.com

34-35 Port-au-Prince couple © arindambanerjee/Shutterstock.com
Yellow sign © Vaju Ariel/Shutterstock.com
Ruins of buildings © Cristian Zamfir/Shutterstock.com
Port-au-Prince tent city © arindambanerjee/Shutterstock.com
36-37 ground crack © koya979/Shutterstock.com
buildings © John T Takai/Shutterstock.com
38-39 Soufriere Hills Montserrat © Photovolcanica.com/
Shutterstock.com
40-41 Lava © Mark Yarchoan/Shutterstock.com
42-43 Volcano Cross-section © George W. Bailey/Shutterstock.com
background © VOOK/Shutterstock.com
Night volcano eruption © Byelikova Oksana/
Shutterstock.com
44-45 background VOOK/Shutterstock.com
Old Faithful © Lee Prince/Shutterstock.com
geyser surrounded by bacteria © Krzysztof Wiktor/
Shutterstock.com
volcano graphic © Matthew Cole/Shutterstock.com
46-47 Eyjafjallajokull Iceland © J. Helgason/Shutterstock.com
Blue Lagoon Iceland © Rolf_52/Shutterstock.com
Background © VOOK/Shutterstock.com
48-49 background parchment © pashabo/Shutterstock.com
50-51 volcano graphic © Matthew Cole/Shutterstock.com
background © VOOK/Shutterstock.com
Buried Church © John Cole/Science Photo Library
52-53 Lava © Mark Yarchoan/Shutterstock.com
Mount St. Helens © neelsky/Shutterstock.com
illustration of Mt. St. Helens © Aaron Rutten/Shutterstock.com
Volcano with clouds © albumkoretsky/Shutterstock.com
54-55 Volcano with clouds © albumkoretsky/Shutterstock.com
Koko Head Volcano Oahu Hawaii © Dhoxax/Shutterstock.
com
Hawaiian islands volcanic hot spot © Gary Hincks/Science
Photo Library
56-57 volcanoes © albumkoretsky/Shutterstock.com
Aerial view of Naples © Vacclav/Shutterstock.com
Plaster casts Pompeii © khd/Shutterstock.com
58-59 Details Giant's Causeway © Horia Bogdan/Shutterstock.com
A'a and Pahoehoe lava © Chris Gallagher/Science Photo
Library
pillow lava Oamaru New Zealand © Avenue/Wikipedia
Giant's Causeway © Horia Bogdan/Shutterstock.com
Basalt Columns Boyabat Turkey © Lagrima/Wikipedia
Pumice © Artography/Shutterstock.com
60-61 Solar system © Luka Skywalker/Shutterstock.com
Olympus Mons © NASA/Wikipedia
volcanic eruption Io © NASA
volcanic domes Venus © NASA/Jet Propulsion Laboratory/
Wikipedia
Moon © NASA/Wikipedia
62-63 nature background © Vectomart/Shutterstock.com
lava and fern © George Burba/Shutterstock.com
grapes © holbox/Shutterstock.com
Lanzarote volcanic landscape © John Copland/
Shutterstock.com
Icelandic moss © Evocation Images/Shutterstock.com
Maui Hawaii © Sekar B/Shutterstock.com
64-65 lava background © AKIllustration/Shutterstock.com
volcanoes © albumkoretsky/Shutterstock.com
66-67 fire background © sgame/Shutterstock.com
68-69 background parchment © pashabo/Shutterstock.com
70-71 background parchment © pashabo/Shutterstock.com

Text

Jenny Slater